Introduction

People have been suffering from eating disorders for many years. However, it is only recently that we have begun to understand more about these problems and how to help sufferers.

This book helps you to understand more about the different kinds of eating disorders. It explains some of the reasons that people may develop problems, and discusses the effect that eating disorders can have on sufferers, their family and friends. It also looks at the help that is available. Each chapter introduces and discusses a different aspect of the subject, illustrated by a continuing storyline. The characters in the story deal with the kind of situations which some people may experience themselves. By the end, you will know more about eating disorders and the way in which they can affect people's lives.

— 1 — Why Do We Eat?

Food is essential for growth and health. But eating is not always about filling an empty stomach.

Food plays a very important role in all our lives. We all need to eat to live. But we do not just eat when we are hungry. Sometimes we may use food as a way of expressing our feelings. We may eat because we are hungry, but sometimes we eat or refuse to eat because we feel unhappy. Eating too much or too little can cause problems.

Food has always been an important part of celebrations, such as birthday parties.

Our choice of what, when and where we eat is influenced by many things. The availability and cost of food is a factor. We may be expected to eat a meal which has been prepared for us. We might eat less or more to lose or put on weight.

At religious festivities, such as Christmas or Diwali, special foods are served in honour of the occasion.

Today there is much emphasis on the need to look after our bodies, by eating healthy foods and by taking enough exercise. This is partly a reaction to the way our eating habits have also changed over the years.

We now tend to eat more 'fast foods' and snacks. Because of this, it is particularly important to make sure that we eat a 'balanced diet'. This means choosing food which contains enough of the substances our bodies need to keep healthy.

WHAT DO YOU KNOW ABOUT

ANOREXIA, BULIMIA AND OTHER EATING DISORDERS

Pete Sanders and Steve Myers

W

FRANKLIN WATTS
LONDON • SYDNEY

This edition published in 2000
© Aladdin Books Ltd 1995

Designed and produced by
Aladdin Books Ltd
28 Percy Street
London W1P 0LD

First published in
Great Britain in 1995 by
Franklin Watts
96 Leonard Street
London EC2A 4XD

Previously published in
hardcover in the series
Let's Discuss.

ISBN: 0 7496 2092 7(hardback)
ISBN: 0 7496 3750 1(paperback)

A catalogue record for this
book is available from the
British Library.

Printed in Belgium

Designer   Tessa Barwick
Editor   Sarah Levete
Illustrators   Mike Lacy
                Liz Sawyer

Pete Sanders is Senior
Lecturer in health education
at the University of North
London. He was a head
teacher for ten years and has
written many books on social
issues for children.

Steve Myers is a freelance
writer who has co-written
other titles in this series and
worked on several educational
projects for children.

The consultant, Maureen
Schiller, has worked
extensively in the field of
eating disorders. She has run
many workshops for young
people on eating disorders.

Contents

HOW TO USE THIS BOOK

The books in this series are intended to help young people to understand more about personal issues that may affect their lives. Each book can be read alone, or together with a parent, teacher or helper, so that there is an opportunity to talk through ideas as they come up. Issues raised in the storyline are explored in the accompanying text, inviting further discussion.

At the end of the book there is a chapter called "What Can We Do?" This section provides practical ideas which will be useful for both young people and adults, as well as a list of the names and addresses of organisations and helplines, which offer further information and support.

▽ Nicky Miller and Joanna Purves met up at Sharon's party.

▽ In the end, Nicky only took a small amount of food and a diet cola.

△ Nicky said no. She felt she had already eaten too much.

▽ Later, everyone helped themselves to food.

▽ After everyone had finished, Sharon put on some music.

SHARON CAN EAT THE SAME AMOUNT OF FOOD AS HER FRIENDS, BUT NOT PUT ON THE SAME AMOUNT OF WEIGHT AS THEY MIGHT.

This is because her metabolic rate – the speed at which calories are burned up – is higher than her friends. Metabolic rate is different from person to person. It can be affected by the amount of physical activity we are involved in at any time. During adolescence, when young people's bodies are changing, they may need greater amounts of food. It is natural for young people to put on some weight as a part of growing up.

TO MANY PEOPLE THE WORD 'DIET' HAS COME TO MEAN A 'SLIMMING PLAN'.

As Nicky's friend has pointed out, many slimming plans promise magical results. The reality is that most people find sticking to slimming diets difficult. Nicky sees herself as overweight and thinks that being slimmer, like the models she sees in the magazines and on TV, would make her happy. But there is no one kind of body which is better than another.

FACT FILE: EATING WELL

All food is made up of chemical compounds, called nutrients. The basic nutrients are proteins, carbohydrates, fats, vitamins and minerals. The different food groups – dairy products, meat, fish, fruit, vegetables and grains – contain different amounts of these nutrients. The body needs enough of each nutrient for energy and growth, and to stay well and fight off disease. The body converts the food we eat into energy, which is measured in units called calories.

– 2 – *What Is An Eating Disorder?*

Eating disorders may seem to be all about food, but deep down they are an expression of the way a person feels.

Everybody's eating behaviour can be affected by the way they are feeling. But this does not mean that everyone will develop an eating disorder. An eating disorder is a way some people find of coping with difficult emotions and situations. They focus their feelings on the way they look, and how and what they eat. An eating disorder is not to do with slimming and wanting to have a 'perfect body'; it is about expressing troubled feelings.

There are three main kinds of eating disorder – anorexia nervosa, bulimia nervosa and compulsive eating.

People who suffer from anorexia, severely restrict the amount of food they eat and try to avoid eating. They become very underweight but the way they see their bodies becomes distorted, so that they believe they are overweight.

People who have bulimia eat large amounts of food – binge eating – but then get rid of it, either by making themselves sick or by taking large amounts of laxatives, which make them go to the toilet. People with bulimia are generally neither very thin nor very large. They are also very concerned about their body size.

Compulsive eaters also binge eat, but they do not try to get rid of it. Many become very overweight. Like someone with bulimia, compulsive eaters often eat without feeling at all hungry.

Some people may eat to try and forget about their unhappiness, although they know that doing this will only makes them feel more miserable.

▽ A few weeks later, Nicky and Joanna were watching TV at Joanna's house.

I USED TO ENJOY WATCHING THIS WITH DAD. I HOPED I'D LOOK LIKE THEM. SOME CHANCE.

I WOULDN'T WANT TO.

WHY NOT? THEY'RE ALL SO GOOD LOOKING.

SO WHAT? THERE'S MORE TO LIFE THAN THAT. ANYWAY, HALF THE TIME IT'S NOT NATURAL.

△ Joanna said she had read that lots of actors and actresses had had cosmetic surgery.

THERE'S LOTS OF THINGS I'D CHANGE ABOUT ME IF I COULD.

I'VE MADE A CASSEROLE. THERE'S PLENTY. ARE YOU GOING TO STAY AND HAVE SOME, NICKY?

THANKS, MRS PURVES, BUT I CAN'T. MUM WILL HAVE SOMETHING READY FOR ME WHEN I GET HOME.

I THOUGHT YOU WERE GOING TO TELL YOUR MUM YOU WERE HAVING TEA HERE.

I FORGOT, OK? I'D BETTER BE GETTING HOME.

▽ Arriving home, Nicky tried to sneak in but her mum heard her.

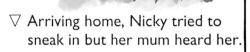

NICKY, YOU'RE LATE AGAIN. I'VE KEPT YOUR TEA WARM FOR YOU. COME AND SIT DOWN.

△ Joanna was puzzled by Nicky's sudden change of mood.

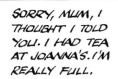
SORRY, MUM, I THOUGHT I TOLD YOU. I HAD TEA AT JOANNA'S. I'M REALLY FULL.

NO, YOU DIDN'T TELL ME. YOU REALLY TRY MY PATIENCE SOMETIMES, YOUNG LADY. WHAT AM I SUPPOSED TO DO WITH THIS?

DON'T WORRY, MUM, I'LL EAT IT.

OK, JAMIE. IT'S GOOD TO KNOW I CAN RELY ON ONE OF YOU, AT LEAST.

▽ Later, Jamie came in to ask Nicky's advice.

WHICH DO YOU THINK I SHOULD TAKE ON HOLIDAY?

△ Nicky went to her room feeling miserable.

THAT'S SILLY, NICKY. SHE WAS JUST ANNOYED AT YOU TONIGHT FOR BEING LATE. SHE DOESN'T BLAME YOU FOR ANYTHING.

WHO CARES? I DON'T WANT TO GO ON HOLIDAY ANYWAY. IT WON'T BE THE SAME WITHOUT DAD.

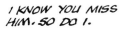
▽ Nicky's mum and dad had separated a few months ago.

I KNOW YOU MISS HIM. SO DO I.

I DON'T KNOW WHY HE HAD TO LEAVE. SOMETIMES I THINK IT'S ALL MY FAULT. I'M SURE MUM THINKS SO.

SHE ACTS LIKE SHE DOES.

9

NICKY HAS LIED ABOUT HAVING EATEN AT JOANNA'S HOUSE BECAUSE SHE WANTS TO AVOID EATING. People with eating disorders are often very secretive. They may go to great lengths not to have to eat, or to hide their bingeing. This might involve lying, or avoiding situations involving food.

IF YOU ARE WORRIED ABOUT YOUR FEELINGS OR BEHAVIOUR AROUND FOOD, TALKING TO A FRIEND OR ADULT CAN HELP. Being honest about how you feel and being aware of the possible problems may prevent an anxiety from developing into a serious concern.

FACT FILE: BEHAVIOUR

This list shows the main behaviour patterns of people suffering from different eating disorders. But people often swing between different types of behaviour.

Anorexics may:	*Compulsive eaters may:*	*Bulimics may:*
• eat extremely little	• binge eat	• binge eat
• pretend they've eaten	• eat constantly	• hide or steal food
• be obsessed with other people's eating habits	• exercise excessively	• eat in secret
• occasionally binge and make themselves sick	• go through strict periods of dieting	• make themselves sick
• occasionally take laxatives	• be moody and irritable	• take laxatives
• exercise excessively	• cry a lot	• exercise excessively
• be moody and irritable	• weigh themselves constantly	• be moody and irritable
• cry a lot		• cry a lot
• weigh themselves constantly		• go through strict periods of dieting
		• weigh themselves constantly

–3– What Kind Of People Are Affected?

"I used to think that it was only girls who worried about food. But two of my mates at school are always worrying about how much they eat. They don't seem to be very happy."

From time to time, everybody may worry about the amount of food they eat. This does not necessarily mean that they have an eating disorder or will develop one. Eating disorders can happen to anyone, at any age, of any race or culture. Although about 90% of sufferers are women and girls, there is an increasing number of men and boys who are affected by eating problems.

There is no one kind of person who is more likely to be a sufferer. It can be difficult to tell that someone has a problem with food, unless they are very underweight.

Today there is much emphasis on outward appearance. More women suffer from eating disorders in societies where there is a lot of pressure from the media to be very slim. It can be very hard to resist the idea that being a certain shape or size will make you happy.

Many sufferers want to be perfect in every area of their lives. Many are very successful, for instance in school or work, but they still have a very low opinion of themselves. They feel that they can never do well enough or be good enough.

▽ The next weekend, Mrs Miller persuaded Nicky to go shopping with her. Joanna went along too.

△ Mrs Miller put the swimsuit in her basket, and turned her attention to Nicky.

◁ Mrs Miller told Nicky she was being silly, but Nicky refused to change her mind.

▽ The three of them went to the department store coffee shop.

▷ Later, Joanna asked Nicky why she had been lying.

1990

TODAY MAGAZINES, TV AND ADVERTISEMENTS BOMBARD US WITH IMAGES OF VERY SLIM WOMEN AND MUSCULAR MEN.

In the past, the fashion was for women to be plump and rounded. In some cultures today this is also the case. Joanna does not think she has to be slim to be beautiful or feel good about herself, but Nicky feels that her self-worth is judged by the way she looks. It is important to remember that each person is unique and special, regardless of body size or shape.

MRS MILLER IS QUITE RELAXED ABOUT HER INTENTION TO BE SLIMMER FOR THE HOLIDAY.

She does not realise that her remarks have made Nicky feel more uncomfortable. Parents can often influence the way their children feel.

CASE STUDY:
MICHAEL, AGED 14

"I used to get teased about being chubby. I began exercising for hours and hardly ate anything. But it made me feel so miserable. I didn't want to go out and couldn't concentrate at school. Mum asked me what was up. She was really nice about it, and didn't make fun of me. We talked about how I was feeling and what I was doing. That really helped."

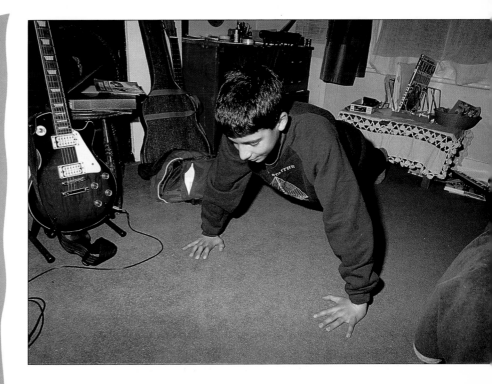

There is no one simple reason why a person develops an eating disorder. The causes are different for different people.

Unlike other illnesses, you cannot 'catch' an eating disorder. An eating disorder is caused by difficult and complicated feelings, and not by physical problems. For many people, it may be a response to an issue or situation in their lives which they find painful and difficult to face. An eating disorder becomes a way of coping with feelings of unhappiness.

It can help if you feel able to express your feelings, instead of keeping them to yourself.

Someone with an eating disorder is trying to cope with emotions which they believe they are unable to deal with in any other way than through their eating behaviour. Such feelings of anger, guilt or sadness may have been locked inside for a long time and the sufferer may not even recognise or understand them. They may have been sparked off by an event such as the break up of a relationship, or changing school or house.

People with an eating disorder may believe that they are to blame for something unpleasant which has happened. They think of themselves as 'bad', and the way that they use food against themselves becomes proof of this 'badness'. Children who have been abused may use food as a way of coping with their unhappiness and confusion.

▽ On holiday, the Millers met Mr & Mrs Thompson and their children, Keith and Kelly.

WOULD YOU LIKE ME TO GET YOU A BURGER?

NO THANKS. I'M NOT VERY HUNGRY.

SHE EATS LIKE A BIRD, BUT SHE STILL INSISTS THAT SHE'S FAT.

I DON'T THINK YOU'RE FAT. YOU LOOK FINE TO ME.

△ Keith's comment caught Nicky off guard. She felt slightly uncomfortable.

WHY DON'T YOU SIT HERE, NICKY?

THANKS, BUT I'D RATHER NOT SIT FACING THE SUN.

▽ When they had their food, the families sat down to eat.

ARE YOU SURE YOU WON'T HAVE SOMETHING? WHY DON'T YOU SHARE MY BURGER?

I SAID I DIDN'T WANT ANYTHING. YOU JUST WANT ME TO BE FAT, DON'T YOU?

THERE, ARE YOU SATISFIED NOW? CAN I GO?

WHY NOT? YOU THINK I'VE RUINED EVERYTHING ELSE.

WHAT ON EARTH'S THE MATTER WITH YOU? DO YOU WANT TO RUIN THE HOLIDAY FOR EVERYONE?

◁ Nicky grabbed the burger and stuffed it in her mouth. She ate it as quickly as she could.

▽ Mrs Miller apologised to the Thompsons for Nicky's behaviour.

> SHE'S HAD THESE SILLY IDEAS ABOUT EATING FOR WEEKS NOW. I DON'T KNOW WHAT TO DO.

> MAYBE THEY'RE NOT SILLY, MRS MILLER. KELLY USED TO HAVE A REAL PROBLEM WITH FOOD.

▷ Kelly told Mrs Miller that a year ago she was worried about her exam results and had practically stopped eating. Her doctor had said she was showing signs of anorexia.

> TALKING ABOUT IT AND UNDERSTANDING WHY I WAS BEHAVING LIKE THAT, HELPED ME TO CHANGE BEFORE IT GOT OUT OF CONTROL.

▽ Back in the hotel, Jamie heard Nicky in the bathroom being sick.

> OH, I DON'T THINK IT'S THAT SERIOUS. NICKY'S JUST BEING DIFFICULT.

◁ But Mrs Thompson told her there might be more to it than that.

> NICKY, ARE YOU ALL RIGHT? WHAT'S WRONG?

> NOTHING, I JUST DIDN'T FEEL TOO WELL. I'LL BE OKAY IN A MINUTE.

▷ In fact, Nicky had made herself sick, to get rid of the food that she had felt forced to eat.

IF A CLASSMATE GOES ON A DIET, IT MAY MAKE OTHER PEOPLE AT SCHOOL FEEL ANXIOUS AND SELF-CONSCIOUS ABOUT THEIR OWN BODIES.
An eating problem can develop if a diet gets out of control. Rather than being a way of losing a little weight, the diet may become the focus of a person's life. This constant preoccupation and concern with food and body image, can be a way of avoiding difficult and unhappy feelings, which the person may not even be aware of.

NICKY IS FRIGHTENED BY KEITH'S FRIENDLINESS.
People who suffer from an eating disorder often dislike themselves so much that they cannot believe anyone else could like them. They find it hard to trust someone enough to allow that person to get close to them.

NICKY DID NOT FEEL IN CONTROL OF THE FOOD SHE ATE SO SHE MADE HERSELF SICK.
Anorexics sometimes lose control over their strict dieting, and eat more than the little they allow themselves. They then may make themselves sick to get rid of the food. Compulsive eaters and bulimics often eat food as a comfort and to blot out feelings but this makes them feel worse about themselves.

—5— What It Means To Have An Eating Disorder

"All I do is think about food, 24 hours a day. At night I can't sleep, and during the day I just feel moody and unhappy."

It can be lonely and confusing to be torn between wanting to eat, and being terrified of eating.

For people with an eating disorder, food becomes the most important thing in their lives, causing them constant anxiety. The success or failure of any particular day is measured by the amount of food they have managed to resist eating, or have actually eaten.

People suffering from an eating disorder may experience strong mood swings which can depend on whether or not the person feels the day has been a 'good' one. For anorexics, this may mean that they have managed to eat as little as possible. For bulimics and compulsive eaters, it may mean that they have not eaten large amounts of food.

It can be very hard for bulimics and compulsive eaters to form close relationships because they feel such a strong sense of guilt and shame about their behaviour. They may believe that nobody else behaves in this way. They often lead very solitary lives because they want to avoid eating or find it difficult to eat in company. Their lives become so dominated by food that they do not feel able to let anyone else into their secretive world. This lack of social contact can lead to further feelings of loneliness and unhappiness.

Sometimes people with an eating disorder have such a strong sense of self-dislike, that they do deliberate damage to their bodies.

▽ A month later, after school, Nicky bumped into Joanna and Sharon.

HI, NICKY. WE WERE JUST TALKING ABOUT YOU. YOU HAVEN'T BEEN OUT WITH US FOR AGES. DO YOU WANT TO COME TO THE PICTURES TONIGHT?

WHAT'S HAPPENED TO HER? SHE LOOKS TERRIBLE.

I KNOW.

NO THANKS. I'VE GOT TO STAY IN AND HELP MUM.

▽ On the way home, Joanna told Sharon she thought Nicky might have an eating disorder.

I THINK NICKY'S TRYING TO AVOID FOOD ALTOGETHER. I KNOW SHE'S LIED ABOUT HOW MUCH SHE EATS.

ONE OF MY SISTER'S FRIENDS HAD BULIMIA. SHE'D HAVE THESE BINGES WHERE SHE ATE LOADS OF FOOD. THEN SHE'D MAKE HERSELF SICK.

△ Nicky overheard them. But she thought that they meant she still looked fat.

▽ That evening, Nicky refused to come down from her room.

I'VE RUNG YOUR DAD. I'M MEETING HIM IN AN HOUR TO TRY TO DECIDE WHAT TO DO ABOUT NICKY. THIS CAN'T GO ON.

I'M REALLY WORRIED ABOUT HER MUM, SHE'S LOST SO MUCH WEIGHT.

▽ After her mum left, Nicky went downstairs. She found Jamie in the kitchen.

I WAS GOING TO BRING YOU UP A SANDWICH. I THOUGHT YOU MIGHT BE HUNGRY BECAUSE YOU DIDN'T HAVE ANY TEA.

I TOLD YOU BEFORE, I DON'T WANT ANY-THING. WHAT DO YOU CARE, ANYWAY?

OF COURSE I CARE. YOU'RE MY KID SISTER. YOU CAN BE A PAIN IN THE NECK, BUT I STILL LOVE YOU.

WELL, MAYBE YOU SHOULDN'T.

IT IS NOT EASY FOR THE FAMILY AND FRIENDS OF PEOPLE WITH AN EATING DISORDER TO COPE. They may want to help but be unsure what to say or do for the best. Tension can build up and they may react in inappropriate ways – perhaps trying to force someone to eat or trying to coax or trick a person into eating.

PEOPLE WITH AN EATING DISORDER ARE OFTEN TORN BETWEEN CONFLICTING EMOTIONS. They may feel that control over their eating gives them power and independence, but they also know that they are not in control of their behaviour. They may feel hungry because their body is physically craving the food it is being denied, but they are also frightened of eating. The obsession with food and body image makes them unhappy, but they feel trapped by it.

CASE STUDY: JENNIFER, AGED 13

"Even though I was starving myself, I was obsessed by other people's eating. I even made them meals. But if anyone tried to make me eat, I'd become so angry. I weighed myself whenever I could. If I had put on even half a pound, I would be thrown into total panic and start to exercise even more."

—6— What Can Happen To The Body?

"I knew I was damaging my body, but I couldn't stop myself. I was really scared though."

Although eating disorders are about feelings, they have physical effects on the body of the sufferer. Most of these disappear in time, once the person is eating regularly again. But sometimes people can do lasting damage to their bodies and some of the physical effects can be very serious if left untreated.

Starving oneself or getting rid of food through vomiting or taking laxatives, upsets the balance of the body. Someone with an eating disorder often feels very tired and physically very weak.

If you have been ill yourself recently, you may understand how if one part of the body is poorly, this can affect the way the rest of the body works. Being healthy means looking after the whole person. The way that we feel about ourselves is a key factor in our well-being. Denying ourselves the food we need, does not just affect our weight. Our minds, as well as our bodies, can be affected. People who are starving themselves often have great difficulty concentrating and lack energy. The effects of extreme weight loss, extreme over-eating, constant vomiting and taking of laxatives can lead to death.

SHE HAS ANOREXIA. SHE'S LOST A LOT OF WEIGHT IN A SHORT TIME. THAT, AND THE OCCASIONAL BOUTS OF VOMITING, PUT A GREAT STRAIN ON HER SYSTEM.

SO WHAT DO WE DO? HOW DO WE GET HER TO EAT PROPERLY AGAIN?

◁ The family persuaded Nicky to see a doctor. She examined Nicky and later spoke to Mr and Mrs Miller.

SHE'LL HARDLY EAT FOR DAYS. THEN ONCE IN A WHILE SHE BINGES AND THROWS IT ALL UP AGAIN. I'VE TRIED EVERYTHING TO MAKE HER SEE SENSE.

NICKY IS VERY UNHAPPY. TRYING TO FORCE HER TO EAT NOW MAY ONLY MAKE MATTERS WORSE.

I THOUGHT IT WAS JUST A SILLY PHASE. I THOUGHT SHE'D TIRE OF IT, AND PULL HERSELF TOGETHER.

△ The doctor told them it wasn't just a question of getting Nicky to eat again. The problem was to do with Nicky's feelings as well.

I'M AFRAID NOT. IT'S GOING TO TAKE TIME AND UNDERSTANDING TO GET NICKY WELL AGAIN. WHAT MATTERS NOW IS FINDING THE BEST TREATMENT.

▽ A few days later, Joanna ran into Jamie and asked about Nicky.

THE DOCTOR'S GOING TO CONTINUE TO SEE HER, BUT SHE'D LIKE NICKY TO SEE A THERAPIST AS WELL.

WE'VE ALL BEEN WORRIED ABOUT HER. WHAT DID THE DOCTOR SAY?

SHE TALKED TO HER FOR A LONG TIME, TO HELP NICKY UNDERSTAND WHY SHE IS BEHAVING LIKE THIS, AND WHAT SHE IS DOING TO HER BODY.

△ The doctor said a therapist would help Nicky to talk about her feelings.

THE WHOLE BODY CAN BE AFFECTED BY AN EATING DISORDER.

The illustration opposite shows some of the physical problems that can result from having an eating disorder, whether it is anorexia, bulimia or compulsive eating.

THE DOCTOR HAS POINTED OUT THE DAMAGE NICKY IS DOING TO HER BODY.

She has lost a great deal of weight which has made her body very weak and less able to work properly. It is not a good idea to lose a lot of weight in a short time, which is why most doctors do not recommend 'crash' diets. Even people who may be very overweight and need to slim for health reasons are advised to do so gradually. This allows the body to adjust to the change slowly.

VOMITING OR USING LAXATIVES TO EXCESS CAN BE DANGEROUS.

When you vomit, you lose many of the nutrients the body needs to stay healthy. Laxatives also have this effect. The physical exertion of vomiting on a regular basis can put a lot of stress on the body.

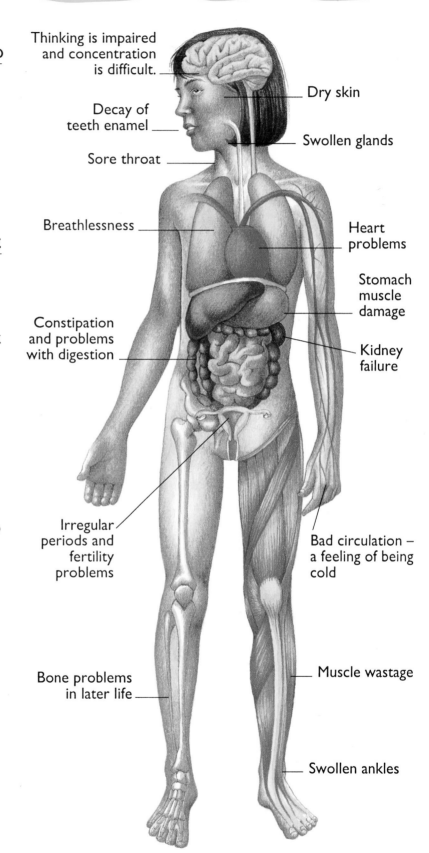

Thinking is impaired and concentration is difficult.

Decay of teeth enamel

Sore throat

Dry skin

Swollen glands

Breathlessness

Heart problems

Stomach muscle damage

Constipation and problems with digestion

Kidney failure

Irregular periods and fertility problems

Bad circulation – a feeling of being cold

Bone problems in later life

Muscle wastage

Swollen ankles

—7— Getting Help

The first stage of getting help is for the sufferer to admit to him-or-herself that there is a problem.

It is difficult for people with an eating disorder to accept that they need help. Once they have done so, they will often feel a great sense of relief. Many sufferers will require some kind of outside help, in addition to the support of friends and family. It is important that sufferers receive the help that they need and as early as possible.

People with an eating disorder may think that their feelings and behaviour are so over-whelming that there is no way that they can ever be helped or recover. But just talking to someone is a good starting point.

They may go to their doctor who might recommend that they see a therapist or counsellor. These are people who are trained to help others talk about their feelings and understand their behaviour. If the doctor considers that the person's life is in danger, hospital treatment may be recommended.

There are many kinds of treatment to help people with eating disorders, but what works for one person may not always work for another. It may take time to find the right kind of support. Different treatments may not be available to everyone in the area they live in. Some treatments may be quite expensive.

▷ Eventually, Nicky had agreed to see the therapist. But it was a few weeks before she felt comfortable talking to her.

I FEEL STRANGE BEING HERE. WHAT DO YOU WANT TO TALK ABOUT TODAY?

ANYTHING YOU WANT TO. WHY DON'T YOU TELL ME HOW YOU'RE FEELING AT THE MOMENT?

IT SCARES ME TO TALK ABOUT HOW I FEEL.

IT'S OKAY TO BE SCARED, NICKY. YOU DON'T HAVE TO TELL ME ANYTHING YOU DON'T WANT TO.

▽ After a few sessions, Nicky agreed that her parents could join some of their discussions.

I'M SO WORRIED ABOUT HER. I DON'T KNOW WHAT TO DO.

NICKY HAS AGREED TO TRY NOT TO LOSE ANY MORE WEIGHT AND TOGETHER WE ARE WORKING ON AN EATING PLAN.

△ They talked for an hour. Gradually, Nicky explained how she'd been feeling since her parents had split up.

WHAT GOOD WILL THAT DO? SHE NEEDS TO BUILD UP HER WEIGHT NOW.

I HOPE MUM AND DAD WON'T BE ANGRY.

I WARNED YOU AT THE BEGINNING THAT SOME THINGS MIGHT BE DIFFICULT FOR YOU TO FACE.

△ The therapist explained that Nicky was using food as a way of coping with her feelings about her father leaving home.

IT'S A START, MR MILLER. THIS ISN'T JUST ABOUT HER WEIGHT. NICKY FEELS VERY CONFUSED AND NEEDS TO FEEL GOOD ABOUT HERSELF AGAIN.

THEY BOTH CARE ABOUT YOU, NICKY. WE ALL JUST WANT YOU TO GET BETTER.

IT IS IMPORTANT THAT THE HELP IS APPROPRIATE FOR THE SUFFERER.

Possible treatments might involve a stay in hospital, or a counsellor may suggest attending a self-help group, or group therapy. Doctors and therapists often recommend keeping a 'feelings and food' diary. Doing this can help people see how particular feelings affect food and the way they eat.

THE THERAPIST HAS WARNED **M**R & **M**RS **M**ILLER THAT THEY MAY HAVE TO TO FACE SOME PAINFUL FACTS ABOUT **N**ICKY'S ILLNESS.

It can also be hard for sufferers because they realise that receiving help might involve their family having to go through some very difficult times. There may be angry scenes. It can be tempting to give up, but this would not make the problem go away.

PEOPLE WITH AN EATING DISORDER ARE OFTEN LONGING TO ASK FOR HELP BUT ARE VERY FRIGHTENED ABOUT WHAT GETTING HELP MAY MEAN.

They may be very worried about other people's reactions if they tell them about their difficulties with eating. They may worry that they will no longer be loved or accepted by the people close to them. But people can be very understanding and supportive. Talking about your feelings can make you feel less isolated and alone.

Sufferers may believe that to accept help will mean them having to give up the one fragment of control they think they have in their lives. They fear that they will become powerless. It can take a long time to build up trust.

The Process Of Recovery

Unlike many illnesses there is no simple and quick remedy for eating disorders. There are no hard and fast rules to follow. It is important to remember that the path of recovery is not all forwards and may take a long time. It could require a great deal of effort and understanding on everybody's part.

Getting better is not always easy. It can be like the board games that young children play – some steps forward, and then a few steps backwards.

Family and friends sometimes feel helpless or impatient. The sufferer may feel under a lot of pressure. It can be tempting to believe that recovery is complete once a person's eating is regular. This may not be the case – the feelings which caused the problem might still need to be dealt with. The person who is recovering may still have feelings of guilt and shame which are difficult to handle.

Sometimes things may seem to be getting better, and then suddenly slip back again. It can help to remember that each day you can start again. With the right kind of help and understanding, progress can be made.

It can be very difficult for someone with an eating disorder to accept that the process of recovery means that he or she needs to continue to eat in a balanced way – this means coming to terms with food, which up until now has been the focus of the problem.

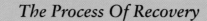

▽ The therapist recommended therapy with other people who suffered from eating disorders.

THANK YOU, NAOMI. WOULD ANYONE ELSE LIKE TO SAY ANYTHING?

I JUST WANTED TO SAY THAT IT'S REALLY HELPED ME HAVING PEOPLE TO TALK TO.

MUM'S TRYING REALLY HARD, BUT SOME THINGS I STILL FIND HARD TO DISCUSS WITH HER

△ Nicky had been attending group therapy for two months.

▽ Nicky had missed some school as a result of her illness. She had only been back a few weeks.

▽ Nicky's mum collected her after the session.

MUM, THIS IS MY FRIEND, NAOMI, I'VE INVITED HER ROUND ON SATURDAY. IS THAT OK?

OF COURSE. I'M VERY PLEASED TO MEET YOU NAOMI.

IT'S GOOD HAVING YOU AROUND AGAIN. I BET IT STILL FEELS STRANGE.

YEAH, I'M GLAD TO BE BACK, BUT IT STILL SEEMS A BIT SCARY.

THERE'S A LOT TO CATCH UP ON.

YOU'LL BE OK. JUST TAKE IT AS IT COMES.

△ Nicky knew they were right.

NICKY IS CONCERNED ABOUT CATCHING UP ON THE SCHOOLWORK SHE HAS MISSED.

Sometimes it is tempting to try too hard. Feeling pressured into being well and becoming your 'old self' again can get in the way of recovery. It does not help to try to rush things, or expect everything to be exactly as it was before the problem began. Recovering from an eating disorder can be a painful process for everybody involved. But people do get well, and do make a complete recovery.

NICKY HAS FOUND THAT IT HAS HELPED HER TO TALK ABOUT HER PROBLEMS WITH PEOPLE WHO UNDERSTAND HER SITUATION.

Talking openly about how we feel can help, but talking about eating disorders can be difficult. It means bringing up emotions which may be distressing. But being able to express feelings is a key part of getting better.

FACTFILE:
HEALTH AND WELL-BEING
The process of recovery may involve:
- learning how to express your feelings and to communicate clearly with others
- recognising patterns of behaviour
- learning to handle setbacks
- trying not to 'run before you can walk'
- allowing yourself to feel OK
- feeling that it is OK to have needs and to express them
- learning how to care for your body
- feeling allowed to be wrong and knowing that you don't have to be perfect

What Can We Do?

People suffering from an eating disorder may need a great deal of care and understanding from those closest to them.

With the right support, people do recover from eating disorders.

Having read this book you will be more aware of the different kinds of eating disorders that people can suffer from. You will understand more about the effect they can have on your life and the lives of people around you.

Anorexia, bulimia and compulsive eating can cause physical problems and a great deal of unhappiness. You may know somebody who has an eating disorder. You may even be experiencing problems yourself. It is important to remember that many people have worries about food and their own self-image at some point in their lives. This does not necessarily mean that they will go on to develop an eating disorder. But it is also important to be honest with yourself and others about your feelings and behaviour.

EATING DISORDERS ASSOCIATION
1st floor
Wensum House
103 Prince of Wales Road
Norwich
Norfolk NR1 1DW
Tel: 01603 621 414 (helpline)
01603 765050 (youthline)
E-mail:
info@edauk.com
Website:
www.edauk.com

Adults and young people who have read this book together may find it useful to talk about their experiences, and how they feel about food and different body images.

With eating disorders, adults may not recognise the problem as serious, until it has become out of control. Sometimes it can be tempting to ignore behaviour which they think is just a 'phase'. It may be difficult for parents to accept that their child is unhappy.

People who are affected by an eating disorder may want to discuss their feelings with someone not directly involved. The organisations listed below will be able to provide further information and support for sufferers, their families and friends.

CHILDLINE
50 Studd Street
London N1 0QW
Tel: 0207 239 1000
Helpline: 0800 1111
E-mail:
reception@childline.org.uk
Website:
childline.org.uk

THE CHILDREN'S SOCIETY
56-89 Margery Street
London WC1X OJL
Tel: 0207 837 4299
Website:
www.the-childrens-society.org.uk

NATIONAL CENTRE FOR EATING DISORDERS
54 New Road
Esher
Surrey
KT10 9NU
Tel: 01372 469493
E-mail:
ncfed@globalnet.co.uk
Website:
www.eating-disorders.org.uk

ANOREXIA & BULIMIA NERVOSA FOUNDATION OF VICTORIA INCORPORATE
1513 High Street
Glen Iris 3146
Victoria
Australia
Tel: (00 613) 885 0318

EATING DISORDERS SUPPORT GROUP AUCKLAND
PO Box 80-142
Greenbay
Auckland
New Zealand

Index

Photocredits
All the pictures in this book are by Roger Vlitos. The publishers wish to acknowledge that all the people photographed in this book are models.